INTRODUCTION TO DESIGN

Understanding the original design of individuals based on Redemptive Gifts

Pat Banks

Other books by Pat:
Loved to Transparency
Which Tree

Copyright Pat Banks

All scripture quotations, unless otherwise indicated, are taken from
Scripture quotations marked (NASB) are taken from the New American Standard Bible®, Copyright © 1960, 1962, 1963, 1968, 1971, 1972, 1973, 1975, 1977, 1995 by The Lockman Foundation. Used by permission.
Scripture quotations marked (AMP) are taken from the Amplified Bible, Copyright © 1954, 1958, 1962, 1964, 1965, 1987 by The Lockman Foundation. Used by permission.
Scripture quotations marked (BBE), (ASV) and (KJV) are taken from the Bible in Basic English, American Standard Version and King James Version respectively. Public Domain.

Please note that Pat Banks' publishing style capitalizes certain pronouns in Scripture that refer to the Father, Son, and Holy Spirit, and may differ from some Bible publisher's styles.

Copyright © 2020 Pat Banks
All Rights Reserved
No part of this book may be reproduced in any form, except for the inclusion of brief quotations in review, without permission from the author/publisher.
Printed in the USA

Contact Information

mail@JimandPatBanks.com

ACKNOWLEDGEMENTS

I want to thank Arthur Burk (www.theslg.com) and JoAnn Arizaga for providing the Body of Christ with such rich and valuable information. Much of what I have learned and tried to communicate in this book has been gleaned from their teachings. They will be pleased to know that several marriages have been saved from dissolution as a result of receiving and applying what each of them has taught.

CHAPTER ONE

WHO ARE YOU?

This is a question we are asked frequently in our interaction with other people. It is a question we often ask ourselves. We find ourselves contemplating that issue at various times throughout our lives. Who am I? Why am I here? Where do I belong? What is my purpose? We answer those questions in different ways at different times, but all of our answers seemingly end up being no more than pictures, if you will, of what we do in life. We might answer with some of the following;

I am (Name)
I am a female/male
I am a wife
I am a husband
I am a mother/father
I am a teacher
I am an engineer
I am an artist
I am a free spirit

The list goes on and on, reflecting the function and imputed value of person who is interacting with the world around them. Their abilities and talents, responsibilities and functions with maybe an occasional attempt at a deeper definition. This question has been asked since the beginning of time. And how it is answered defines what we consciously think of our life, relationships, and especially our sense of fulfillment and realized dreams.

As believers, we would probably add Child of God, Born Again, perhaps also an adherent to the teachings and doctrines of the religious denomination we are a part of, and a few others we have learned.

Ephesians 2:10 has these to add to the mix

I am His work of Art
I am a spiritually transformed person ready to be used for Good Works
I am near and dear to Christ
I am set apart
I am dedicated to the presence of Christ
I am part of the body being built together into a dwelling place for God.

Which of these lists generally govern your life, actions and relationships? Even if we are able to say that the second list is something we currently walk in, many times it is hard to fit it in to the things of everyday life. Both lists are true, and both are absolutely needed, and together they begin to answer the first question of Who

Are You. They are however, not complete by any stretch of the imagination, but a good start on the journey.

WHY AM I HERE

As we look at this question, we have to consider the answers to the first list of statements. It is predictable that our answer to the question of, Why Am I Here? will almost assuredly revolve around those answers.

Being a Mother comes with certain functions that are required in order to fulfill that responsibility. It requires sacrifice, multi-tasking, healing hurts, feeding, clothing, discipline and on and on. So, a Mother is here to raise and guide children to becoming functioning adults and productive, law-abiding citizens who are responsible, socially acceptable humans.

Being a Teacher requires responsibility as well. It requires preparation, organization, and education. It requires patience, ingenuity, discipline, creative thinking. It will require encouragement and consistency as it deals with students. So, a Teacher is here to help students become equipped with the knowledge to achieve skills that will empower them for their lives.

An Artist requires practice, lessons, and vision to produce a piece that will affect people in a way that expresses something from the vision of the artist. Whether it be visual art, music, writing or whatever medium is used.

As you can see all of the first list would have the question of Why Am I Here answered by defining what each one is required to do. Sadly, this is where most people stop at walking in their purpose until life situations change and they have to re-adjust what they do. We are not what we do, although who we are is generally reflected in what we do.

There are many more titles people wear every day that they use to define themselves. They do not, however, give a glimpse into the heart of the person and why they were created. Yes, there may be fulfilment and purpose that comes from what they do, but that does not answer, "Why they are here?" Those are simply outward expressions of the inward person.

From a more spiritual standpoint, people can know who Christ says they are created to be when they are born again. However, knowing this as truth and knowing how that works out in everyday life is not always easy. And this is where the difficulty becomes more apparent. This is who Jesus says that I am, but does that answer these questions. Why am I here? Where Do I fit? What is my purpose?

WHY ARE THESE QUESTIONS IMPORTANT

OUR LIFE-----IT'S BIGGER THAN US.

Everything we do, everything we are is affecting the Body of Christ. We were created to live joined to a larger body, functioning together to reveal who Jesus is to the world around us.

> Romans 12:5 Amp. *So, we who are many, are [nevertheless just] one body in Christ, and individually [we are] parts one of another [mutually dependent on each other]"*

All of the above leads us to more questions. One of those questions might be, Does God really give people their purpose? Yes, He does. We see Him calling out and establishing design/purpose throughout the scriptures. Here are some examples.
1. Adam & Eve: Created to walk in intimacy with the Father, while caring for the Garden and taking dominion over the earth.
2. Jeremiah was called a Prophet to the nations set apart in his mother's womb.
3. David was anointed to be King when he was a boy. Long before He was king

4. Mary the Mother of Jesus had her purpose shown to her by an Angel
5. Paul said his determined purpose was to Know Jesus intimately and to preach Gospel
6. JESUS KNEW HIS PURPOSE, He was coming to reconcile all things to His Father.

So how do we find our created design, our purpose, our identity and reason for living? Hopefully, the following will offer at least some introductory thoughts to help you on that journey.

Many people use personality tests to try to help them figure out their life. Many of these are excellent in what they are trying to do. However, personality and design are different things altogether. It is my belief that our design is the lens we look at life through from our conception and our personality develops around it based on life circumstances and interactions. Our personality can change throughout our lifetime, but our design remains the same. It can mature and develop but it is still our fundamental way of processing life. Understanding our design, the way we are shaped to view life, can help us come into agreement with our purpose.

Here is one example that might help get a picture of this. In a nursery of 2 & 3-year-old children, there are several obvious types;

There are those who build towers and those who knock them down. There are those who cry over everything and those who want to hug everyone. There are those who sit in the corner and look at a book and those who want to tell everyone what to do.

We have said look at their personalities, but what if it is actually their design that will set the course for how they view and respond to life. Then parenting, birth order, life events, and culture begins to shape their outward personality to relate to the world around them.

Here are some questions which might help start the design and purpose discovery process.

1. What brings you life when you engage it?
2. What leaves you tired?
2. How do you respond to weaknesses in others?
3. How do you respond to weaknesses in yourself?
4. What do your friends and family see in you?
5. Do you prefer being alone or with people?
6. What are your natural tendencies, likes and dislikes?
7. What do you dream about?
8. Which part of the body are you created to be and how do you express that?

CHAPTER TWO

REDEMPTIVE GIFTS

A helpful resource for finding the answers to these questions and more can be found in a teaching called Redemptive Gifts. This teaching addresses design and not personality. The purpose of this book is to give an overview of the Redemptive Gift teaching to help you move down the road to finding answers to your design.

Here is a little background on Redemptive Gifts. In the early 80's a man by the name of Bill Gothard developed a study called Motivational Gifts. These gifts were based on the gifts listed in Romans 12:6-8 KJV. He taught them as gifts that were the basic motivation of a person. Years later several other groups began to expand on this premise. Arthur Burk has done extensive teaching on these and it is his work, as well as that of JoAnn Arizaga, that has shaped much of the background behind this book. Doug and Katie Fortune wrote on them.

Again, this book is an overview of why identity and design are so important and how to begin the process of determining your wiring.

Arthur Burk and a group of people were studying the seven gifts and began to look at other lists of seven in the bible. They began to see many of the same characteristics showing up across the corresponding numbers in several of the lists of seven found in the Bible. Gathering all the first items in each list of seven formed group of characteristics to investigate. From this study they found some characteristics that seem to correspond to different types of people. As God is a God of order and design, and nothing is happenstance with Him, it is not difficult to see that He would use the same design in building His body.

The list of the seven days of creation will be used in this narrative to show the various design gifts in people. While the gift names correspond with the Gifts in Romans, those titles have different connotations than you would normally ascribe to them. So, try to set aside your definitions to simply see the similarities between them and the gifts. Try not to put those labels on the attributes of each design.

Design has a different origin and function which is not as easily seen. Design is the thumbprint of God on an individual the moment they are conceived. This thumb print is like a lens that they view events of life through and how they respond to them. It is their piece of God's puzzle for fitting His body together, each having a different function and expression of it. The thumbprint or design does not have to be taught how to function, just as a foot or a hand under normal circumstances does not have to be taught to be what they were created to be. They just are. The Bible talks about body parts and how some are to be seen and some are not. It is the same with Redemptive Gifts (Design gifts), as you will see.

Somebody told me just this past week that because my husband and I help people clean the junk out of their lives that our function in the body must be the liver. The liver is obviously not very glamourous organ, but good luck living without one that is fully functional. That's not all we do in the context of personal ministry, but we certainly don't aspire to also be the spleen and the pre-frontal cortex of the brain all at the same time.

The gifts will not be referred to by their titles in Romans 12:6-8 as does Arthur Burk, et al. For the purpose of this overview, the Day of creation which corresponds to the gift will be used to show some of the characteristics of the gift in people.

When looking at the days of creation you will notice that the order of their creation was not random. Each day provided something the next day needed. The same is true with the gifts. They have an interdependence with each other for them to be able to flourish as designed. None of them were designed to stand alone, just like the body parts are designed to work together. It is also true that even as no part of the body is to be devalued, neither is any of the gifts more or less important than another. Some of the benefits to understanding the gifts are as follows:

1. That you will see and appreciate an element of the Father you have not been able to see before. When we begin to see the gifts in each other as an expression of the nature of God, we can begin to receive each other as gifts and also understand the Father better. It may be that if we don't care for one of the gifts in operation, we may have difficulty with the Father when we see Him reflecting that gift.

2. That you personally see how you reflect your heavenly Father. You already look like Him. Some of you just don't know it. You may know it, but you don't see how *they, those other people,* look like Him, It's not a label. It's not a box to put people in. It's not an excuse to say, "Oh, they're *"that"*, well no wonder they think that way." It's none of that. It *is* another opportunity for the Father to get closer to us and for us to finally begin to see how other people operate as they do. It's also not an excuse to stay immature. It's not an excuse to say, "Well it's just the way I am." It *is* a chance to say, "Wow, I'm really immature in this area and I can grow." Or to realize we are created to reflect a part of the

Father and it may look different than others and that is okay.

3. Redemptive gifts allows us the tools to extend grace to people where we haven't been able to in the past. If we can understand how each of us are wired, we won't get offended as easily. It gives us the ability to say, "He didn't know how he was responding, so how I saw it might have been skewed. He was just responding out of the way he was wired, and I took it wrong because of the way I'm wired."

The Word says in Proverbs 22:6 KJV,

> *"Train up a child in the way he should go, then when he's old, he won't depart from it."*

How many of you have raised children and had them seemingly depart? How many of you departed for a while? Not literally, of course. There are some translations that say, "According to his bent." I believe it means according to the design of God in them that is the filter through which they process life.

I believe that those of us in the church have raised people according to what we believe the Christian standard should be and it is founded in what we like, what is easiest for us to get along with.

We may have even extended it so far as to say, this is what a Christian should look like, but what happened with that is we went overboard. We dressed boys in blue pants and white socks and black shoes and short haircuts and white shirts. Girls wore no makeup and wore long skirts. Why? Because the only thing we knew was to change the outward actions and appearance of people in order to make them conform to an image we had of what a Christian should look like and behave like. We call that homogenization; everyone must conform to an established norm. (This example is not intended as a criticism just an observation.) As a result, we have had generations of people growing up and walking away from God and the church because it refused to accommodate who they were created to be and how they chose to express it.

There was a time when a young man would have been thrown out of the church because he had long hair. There was a time and it still exists in some denominations, when having a tattoo meant you were going to Hell. And there are still some that think that way. We have tried to raise them to become something they were never designed to be because that was our idea of what was right. More often than not, we tried to raise them to look, act and think like us. We didn't understand how to raise them according to their bent, their design, which always left them frustrated and disillusioned with the Church.

For those of you with little ones, imagine what would happen if you began to learn and to watch how your child responds, how they see life, and you began to parent them according to *their* bent. You encourage them to function in how they're wired, and you could train them how to mature in that design. You would begin to help them understand, "Jesus made you this way and it's good. Yes, we need to mature in some things. We'll work on some things, but He loves the way you're wired."

Then for the few years that you have them with you, they are being raised with a genuine understanding that Jesus loves how they're made and created. He's been forming them and shaping them to become the absolute best representation of Himself in them, and He's really proud of them. If that would become our model instead of the model we've had, wouldn't that be awesome? It would change the whole culture.

So that's the background of Redemptive Gifts. If you try to tell a blind person that the sky is blue, but in their mind, they think it's purple, you can beat them into submission that the sky is blue, but their view is still going to be that the sky is purple. Right? They don't have any other truth. But if their eyes are opened, and they can see, they will understand the sky is blue. If you try to change people who believe the sky is purple and you are determined it's green, you may get them to say, "Fine, ok, I submit." But you will never have changed the heart into agreement with the truth. The decision that has to be made is do I want to mature and am I willing to look at my weaknesses and strengths, as well as accept those in others.

Now let's begin to look at the characteristics of the gifts and what they might look like in a person. Each of the following chapters will be devoted to a different gift showing the similarities in function between the gifts in Romans 12:6-8 and the days of creation in Genesis. While these are not absolutes, the pattern is what is to be seen.

The gifts, even as the days of creation, have an order to them that is required for each of them to function well together. Each day of creation was built upon the previous day.

So, in other words, order was required, that had to be established, dark and light had to be separated and the earth had to be revealed in order for the rest of creation to exist. Does that make sense? For instance, without gravity, where would we be? We *need* the order of creation.

CHAPTER THREE

DAY ONE – PROPHET

The first gift is the Prophet Redemptive. What happened on the first day of creation? The Word says, "The spirit of God hovered over the deep, it was without form, it was void." There was chaos. That's what the Spirit saw as it hovered over the deep.

What happened on the first day? God saw chaos and He spoke, order came and eliminated chaos, and light came. Light and dark were now separated.

Before anything can happen, to change any situation, any person, any event, light has to come. What does that mean? There has to be a separation between darkness and light. Darkness can look like this in individuals: "I don't get it. I don't see it. I don't understand. This is too hurtful. This is too painful." That can look like darkness. But when light comes, it separates the truth from a lie, hi-lighting the truth will naturally bring order. And that's what happened on the first day of creation. Order came. Had that not happened, it wouldn't have mattered what else was created, because everything would have been in a state of chaos and darkness; and without light and order nothing can live.

The Prophet design gift is not one who sees and foretells the future. It's not one who gives prophetic words, although they could move in the gift of Prophecy. That's not what we're talking about here.

In this instance we're talking about people who are absolutely wired from birth to see everything in terms of black and white, good or bad, right or wrong. They say what they see. If there's an issue going in a relationship, a business or a church, they are the first to see it and are generally the first to give an opinion. They see the problem and they speak to it and they want it to be settled. They separate chaos, just like the Father did. They're problem solvers. One of their greatest frustrations is seeing a problem, seeing a solution but having no input into resolving the problem. Their words carry great authority when they are operating in the fullness of their design, even as the Word on the first day of creation.

Validation: Positive feedback is extremely important to a Prophet gift. You say, "Well everybody needs validation." Here's the difference. Prophets need it at their core because at this point in creation nothing else had been created. So, it's a design gift that basically stands alone, to some degree. Because it's always out there, always separating light and dark. It's always cutting through. Therefore, it can feel very alone. Knowing they are accepted, and getting validation, does not mean flattering words. Prophets will see through that in an instant. But to have the knowledge that someone says "Thanks, that was right on." That's the difference. Or, "Yeah, we need *you* to do this." It is really important.

Another characteristic is their view of right and wrong—there is no gray. Actually, the Lord showed me the distance between right and wrong, black and white, is not gray, it is GRACE. This is either right or this is wrong.

Here is an interesting observation about a Prophet's belief system. It is easy to subtly believe that if someone repents, it is not true repentance until they fully understand the depth of what they have done and the consequences of it. It can't be true repentance if you don't fully grasp the depth of what you've done, especially if it was to me. You know what the Father says? "Oh, just like I treat you?" "Oh..." Because how many times have, we repented without even a glimmer of the depth of what we've have done to Him? There is no gray. There is no compromise because that's the way we're designed to see. But we must learn to extend grace – even to ourselves.

The Word says,

> *"The word of God is living and active and sharper than any two-edged sword, piercing to the division of soul and of spirit, of joints and of marrow; it judges the thoughts and attitudes of the heart."* Hebrews. 4:12

That's what the Prophet will do. There are times they will go into situations and someone's believing a lie and they just *whack*, straight through the lie. Prophets in their immature state can be very quick to judge. Because their words carry authority they must mature to learn when to speak and when to be silent.

Prophets are generally innovative. Always looking for new ways to do things. They generally have new ideas in great quantity. They continually want to try new things, create new models, make things better. Prophets can easily get bored with maintaining things.

Biblical examples; Elijah, Peter, Ezekiel, Caleb, and Miriam.

Peter is the easiest to see in the Prophet Redemptive Gift. He was always the first to speak. The first to come up with a plan. The first to repent and run out ahead. You will note he still exhibited these characteristics after Pentecost but for the most part they were matured.

CHAPTER FOUR

DAY TWO - SERVANT

The second gift listed is the Servant Redemptive. On the second day of creation God created the atmosphere. It is called the firmament and is an essential ingredient for life to exist. He set the boundaries separating the heavens from the earth and the waters above and below. The waters and the air are necessary for the sustenance of life. They cleanse and provide elements for the cycle of life.

Let's look at the characteristics of creation on the second day as it relates to the Servant gift. The servant is the atmosphere. Water is contained in the atmosphere. Oxygen is contained in the atmosphere. What could grow on earth if we didn't have those components of the atmosphere? Nothing would survive without them. Is it seen? No. Does it promote itself? Does it run around going, "Hey, look at me? I'm the air." But without it, nothing could exist. I want you to see, as we talk about these things, we're not talking about an order of importance, because you could not have any of them without the others. And they're absolutely critical for things to work properly.

The servant is life-giving. The servant is cleansing, why? Because water is cleansing. It's necessary for things to grow. It's the unseen support system that makes everything work. The servants are those people that don't need promotion, they don't need to be up front, they don't need to have power, they have absolutely no desire for power. They want to build a platform for people to succeed.

Servant wired people are atmosphere people at their core because they love a peaceful, homey, accepting, casual atmosphere.

Absolutes: They believe a peaceful, casual atmosphere means everyone is happy. "If we all could just dial down, and take a deep breath…" They will run around, until they mature, trying to keep everybody dialed down, and it doesn't work. Not that way.

They have an ability to go into deep places of defilement and cleanse it because of who they are, there's an anointing for them to do that. They can sit with people that are so defiled and it just doesn't bother them. They're the people who love to work with the homeless. They're the people who work with the drug addicts. The prostitute doesn't bother them. They just find it fun to go down and work with the broken and outcast. They love it. They're trying to establish an atmosphere of success around them. They have that responsibility.

Servants are truly those who don't mind being background people. They love building a platform for success for others to grow and find fruitfulness in their own lives. They are like the atmosphere in that they are always there and needed, even if you don't see them. They are also very family oriented.

Servants seem to have great authority in spiritual issues regarding life and death. Jesus said "If you want to be great in the Kingdom of God, you must become a servant of all. Wow, that is a huge statement. Perhaps it is because of the natural humility most Servants walk in that they can walk in the level of authority in spiritual matters.

Biblical examples: Esther, Joseph (husband of Mary), Barnabas.

Have you ever thought about Joseph, the husband of Mary? I mean, how many men, in our society, would think it was manly to marry a woman who's pregnant with someone else's child, who claims to have not had sex with anybody and your name is not hardly mentioned in the whole story. What strength was that in the very nature of that man. He was a Redemptive Servant and everything within him was, "Yes, Father. I'm going to make a platform for her. For she's highly exalted. I'm not challenged, I'm not threatened. I don't need a place. I don't need to be seen. I just get the privilege of coming around and making an atmosphere for her and for that young man to grow." That's real strength, guys.

CHAPTER FIVE

DAY THREE – TEACHER

The third gift is the Teacher Redemptive.
What was created on the third day? Even though Earth was there on the first day, it was covered by water, seemingly without form or definition. On the third day the waters were given boundaries so the earth could sustain life on its solid surface. What do you think of when you think of the ground? Solid. How many of you want to walk around on squishy ground? You don't. You want firm ground. If I am going to build a house it is going to be on firm ground. I want to know that it is solid and that is the Earth. The Earth is the solid foundation.

What does it contain? It is the soil that holds nutrients until they are needed and ready to be released. It contains the fruit. It contains the seed for life. If order hadn't been established, if the atmosphere wasn't there, what's in the Earth would not have mattered because it could not be nurtured. It could not be brought forth. But that is the design of the Teacher. They are the ones that are designed to hold the deep truths of God and release them in their season. The earth also holds magnetic points at its poles so that compasses (truth detectors) work to help guide you.

Teachers generally process internally. They think, they hold thoughts. They're mulling things over in their mind. They're trying to figure things out. Why? Because they are absolutely determined that when they make a decision, it's going to be right. And once they make that decision, it doesn't really matter what else you tell them. It takes an act of God to get them to change their mind. Because that's the way they're wired. Now, can they mature? Yes. Do they mature? If they want to. Because in any of these gifts, in order to mature it is required for you to determine that you're not always right. Then being willing to go before the Lord and asking, "Is this an immature area in me that you want to mature?"

Let's see some Absolutes. They don't make decisions quickly and don't believe automatically something new without examining it and verifying it. They may receive new truths slowly. It's like, "Okay, I hear you, but I'm not sure I'll believe you until I've researched it enough to know that it's true. Once I've decided it's true, then it's true."

Now look at this in relationship to the Father. How many of you have ever thought that the Father was slow to make a decision? Slow to intervene on your behalf. Have you ever believed that? "Well, Lord, can't you do something?" And he's saying, "Mm-hmm, and it's in the soil and it's sitting there and pretty soon, in the right time, I'm going to release what needs to be released so that life can come from it."

We planted a garden; well I guess you could call it a garden. It looked like what was outside the garden when the Garden of Eden was created, and we did not bring dominion to it, therefore it did not produce. You look at that, and the Father's going, "If I release it too soon it's going to look like that." The teachers know how to hold the truths of God. They know how to hold the truths of life and to trust and wait.

Another absolute is they want to understand everything. Knowledge is absolutely important for them. Teachers can get on the computer and they can be researching one thing and four hours later they have been to 100 different sites and learned 25,000 other things in the meantime.

I get on the computer; I find what I want, and I shut it down. Unless I'm playing Solitaire, at which time I can stay because I'm just black and white. I don't have to learn anything if I don't want to. But they can because knowledge is their power. Their validity is that they know. They may not always tell you that they know, but they know they know. This friend of ours says, "Teachers don't think they're right all the time. They know they're right all the time." Now, that's not a pride issue. I want you to understand that it's not necessarily pride. It's the very internal working of God within them that has set them to not be easily swayed. The hard part for them is that they have to begin to mature and allow the Lord to show them when they're wrong, so that they can allow Him to mold them in His image.

Teachers want truth and accuracy. (Your decision can only be as good as the information you have to make it, which is especially important if it involves a lot of money.) Teachers at their core are designed to be searchers of knowledge and truth. They are designed to keep things in order and in clarity and accuracy. They want to make sure all of the facts are presented in order to make a good decision.

Biblical examples of this gift would be Isaiah, Luke and Mary (mother of Jesus)

Luke was a physician. His account of the life of Jesus in his Gospel was by far the most detailed of the four. He was careful to lay out the factual occurrences. There is an order and an exactness to his account.

CHAPTER SIX

DAY FOUR - EXHORTER

The Fourth day of creation is the Exhorter.
What happened on the fourth day of creation? God set the sun, the moon, the stars in their place. Why did we need the sun, the moon, the stars? It would have been awfully dark without the sun, the moon, and the stars, wouldn't it? On the fourth day of creation, God set patterns and order and light into dark places. He established a principle for us that in Him there is always light. He says in Him there's no darkness. The Father says, "I've established light as we go. Light for the night season, light for the day season.

The sun and the moon are set in place and establish the distinction between day and night. They manage the tides and separate night from day. The stars are a beautiful sight in the night sky, and we love to look at them. They're beautiful. Stars are a compass. Sailors have used the stars to navigate trackless wasteland and vast oceans long before there was a GPS. You can follow the compass. You can follow light. The Father used the light, the star, to guide the wise men. That's what Exhorters are designed to do in the order of creation. They set a path and you can follow them. Exhorters and designed to be seen.

What are the exhorter characteristics? They bring light wherever they go. We say they're the party people. They're a party waiting to happen. Right? They don't have a problem being seen. In fact, "Why wouldn't you want to see me? I'm wonderful! Come on guys! What's not to like?" That's the way they think. They don't mean it in pride. It's just, "Come on! Let's lighten up a little bit and have some fun." Why? Because if we had the prophet, the servant, and the teacher, but no light all of you would be really tired of life quickly. We can get heavy, dark, critical, judgmental, and victim quickly. But when you have a mature exhorter walk in and go, "Hey guys! Have I got an idea for you!!!" You're going to want to follow them.

They love to be seen. They love to lead and be in front. It's just who they are. They love a challenge. They love to go. They don't know why you wouldn't want to follow them. They also can show off God's extravagance. When an exhorter is mature, they can show the extravagance of God because that's what the light does. It shows off the full nature, the full character of God. And as we are walking through this world, it isn't just about us performing our duty, it's about coming together to reflect the fullness of who our God is. And they reflect His glory. They draw people to them. Exhorters are like Pied Pipers. People love exhorters. They love to follow them. They love to be around them. Why? They're fun!

If they're immature and it remains all about them, people don't stay around them. They'll leave because it turns out to be all about them.

What are the main values of the exhorter? Fun, spontaneity, their passion. Whatever they're drawn to is absolutely the most important thing in the world. "Why wouldn't you want to fulfill my passion? Why wouldn't you want to help fulfill my idea? This is the most important thing that there could ever be in the entire world!" That's the way they're wired. They see it. They're grabbing hold of it. It's awesome. Let's go for it. It's their baby. It's their dream. They're going to build it.

Encouragement. They're encouragers. When they're in a good place, they're just like, "Come on! You can do this!" When they're not in a good place, not so much. But when they are, they're just an encouragement to be around. Because it's like finally somebody's not so stinking heavy. It's not so sad. It's not so hard. It's fun. And we like to be around those people.

They are Innovators. They're always moving forward. They want to lead and shed light for people to follow and enjoy. They can look like a Prophet, because they are creating new ideas.

They are great at teamwork and networking. They can get people to work together. Exhorters are always looking for ways to connect people and do things. That's the way they're wired. They love celebrations. All through the Old Testament we see celebration, celebration, celebration, party. New testament: Jesus, party, party, party, party with the lost, party. Didn't He? He showed us what an Exhorter looks like. We need to lighten up a little bit.

The sun, moon and stars are necessary for life to grow. They are placed in the middle of the creation story. This is the high point. They have to give life and light to all of the other gifts. Without them the other gifts can become too heavy, dark, judgmental, critical, self-focused, and just hard. Life becomes hard. God put them right in the middle so He can light everything.

Biblical examples are Moses, Jeremiah, and Paul.

I had trouble with Jeremiah being an exhorter because initially I thought he was wired as a prophet. Finally, I realized how many Prophets do I know who would lay naked before a dung heap and really not care? I don't know many. But I know a lot of Exhorters who it wouldn't bother at all. If you look at Jeremiah's life, he didn't care. He just was out there, "Okay, I'm going to do this. God said to do it, so here I go!" And the words he said were prophetic words, but the way he operated, he just brought revelation and light.

CHAPTER SEVEN

DAY FIVE-GIVER

The Fifth day of creation is the Giver.
On the fifth day of creation the birds and the fish came to be, things that reproduced of themselves, laying eggs or gestating internally. Life began to be produced which required a joining together and nurturing of that life. Well, you realize, if things could not reproduce, we wouldn't last very long on this planet. However, the reproduction of this creation required life blood to flow. The birds of the air and sea animals tend to nurture their young. They have an innate sense of long-term generational reproduction.

The Giver is the hardest to pick out. The reason is they are probably the most, to some degree, comfortable in their own skin. They aren't easily impressed by you or me. They really don't need a lot of external fluff. That's why we have to have the givers. They're those people that can birth new things. They're the people that can take a concept or an idea that needs to be done and they can take that thing and bring it to life. They literally can bring the lifeblood needed to cause something to come into being. Things such as businesses, relationships, ideas, money,

If you're around a Giver for very long you'll hear, "I have an idea for a new whatever. I want to create something that will reproduce" Why? Because they're always wanting to birth something. It may be to birth a vision, song, business, or the power of God in a person's life. But there's always this need to be birthing something new. The difference between a Giver and a Prophet or Exhorter in this area is that they are doers. They invest themselves in the birthing of the new thing. Prophets see and declare it; Exhorters see it and want everyone on board to do it. But Givers are like "I Got this"

Givers are not necessarily the people who give. They can be the stingiest people you have ever known. They will give wherever they see it will bear fruit. They're more than likely not going to be the ones giving to the homeless on the street. But they would give to a place where they see fruit being born to help the homeless. They are wise. They're the steward in the Parable of the Talents. They're the ones that got the whole shebang. They're wise with their financial investments. They're wise where they invest their time and energy. The first place where an investment is to be made is in the Kingdom. Expanding and birthing the Kingdom in today's culture is absolutely essential to the body of Christ

There is an anointing on the Giver to make a lot of money. They ought to be drawing wealth to themselves. That's what givers are designed to do. "How do I sow and how do I reap? What's beneficial and what's not?" What would we do without it? There would be nothing fruitful coming.

They want to be in the loop. They don't have to be in control, but they want to know what's going on because they're always checking out, "Is this going to bear fruit?"

They want gratitude, moderation, self-discipline. Their value is that you be a good steward of the resource you're given, and if you're not they wonder what's wrong with you. "How can you not use this right?" They're always birthing and love future planning. If you don't have a plan for long-term reproduction and lineage, there has to be something wrong. There's got to be a plan. They're direct. They're generally not moved by the emotion of the situation. They prune away things that will inhibit growth.

Biblical examples are Abraham, Jacob, Job, and Matthew.

God told Abraham to go and that because God would give him a blessing that all the families of the earth would be blessed through. He gave the power of generational blessing to the giver.

CHAPTER EIGHT

DAY SIX - RULER

The sixth gift is the Ruler Redemptive.
What did God do on day six? He made man and he said, "Here's why I put you here: take dominion." I had an interesting thought. Sometimes I have thoughts that I don't have answers for. This is one of those. Well I do kind of have an answer. Why did He tell them to take dominion after He had put them in a perfect garden? It was like the Lord said, "The dominion wasn't for the garden. The dominion was for the world outside the garden." And we have believed that our dominion is operated within the confines of a church. It was intended to be used to subdue the works of the enemy and bring order to the world yes in the church but mainly outside it.

What happened on that day? Man began to learn. He was given authority. "Name the animals." How many of you would like that to be your first assignment of God? "I want you to name everything that walks in front of you." And you had never seen them before. And man is supposed to do that, why? That's that day of creation. They are designed for order, structure, plans, build, take authority, get the job done. That's the way they're wired.

I happen to believe that many of the stories of the Old Testament we don't like because of God being a Ruler. How many of you have ever struggled with the idea that a loving, caring, precious God that we serve could open the ground and swallow up thousands of people at a time? You've never had a problem with that? I've had a problem with that. If I really want to get on a gut level I can say, "Well He's God, he can do anything." But in my core, there's this thing that goes, "Oh, I'm not sure about that. I mean what kind of God would do that?" And don't we hear people asking that all the time?

God is a Ruler. I believe God would say, I will build my Kingdom and the gates of Hell will not prevail against it. I had it set in motion before I created the Earth and I'm going to build it. Right now, the most important thing to me is not the emotions and care of how people are going to view me. It's going to be to get the job done, because I know what is best."

In the midst of all that, He had a plan, a plan for redemption. He had a plan to take care of it. But right then, He did not consider what people would think. He was going to build the structure of the Kingdom. And that's what Rulers will do. If you've ever worked for a boss that's a Ruler, you feel like he could care less about his people, just get the job done. "What do you mean you're working 48 hours?

I need you to work 60, or 80, or 100 hours! Whatever it takes! We've got to get the job done." We have to step back and realize what's important to them and how we can begin to relate to them in a way that lets them know we value them without coming under their particular mindset for us.

Without Rulers, we would have difficulty building structure. They're wired to bring order in structures, to make things come together so they are sustainable. Have you ever been part of a group where nobody can lead? Do you know how hard it is to get a job done if nobody will take over and say, "We need to do this, this and this, and here's how it needs to happen." It's so stinking frustrating. You just want to throw in the towel. We need rulers. We need people who take dominion and stand in authority. Yes, they need to mature. Yes, they need to have hearts that are more sensitive to the hearts of people, but we need to honor Rulers.

We don't need a lot of Rulers. Rulers are so strong it doesn't take a lot of them to get things in order.

Mature Rulers are incredibly needed and successful in the business world. Because they can take dominion, they can get things done that others aren't able to do. They are often misunderstood because their focus is on what needs to be done. They are often judged as being ego centric and without a lot of compassion.

Biblical examples, Noah. What other gift is going to hear God say, "Build this thing you've never seen before, you don't know what it looks like, but you've got the plan. Work the plan." I don't care what anyone else on the Earth thinks, I'm going to work the plan. And respond with, "Okay. Everything is going to come into place. We're *building* the boat."

CHAPTER NINE

DAY SEVEN - MERCY

And the seventh day of creation is the Mercy. God did everything, He put all the jobs in place. He got everything producing. He got everything working together, and then he said, "Now that I've done it, let's all rest. The Mercy gift was the day when God said, now that you've seen all this, now that I've given you dominion, now that I've done this, I want you to understand how to live from a place of rest in me." None of this was designed to be hard. None of this was designed to be difficult for you. You already have everything you need to do this. Was there anything that Adam wasn't given? Was there anything that Adam needed for life that he wasn't given?

No. Everything that he was given was all he needed. He had the perfect spouse, the perfect provision, the perfect place to live. He had the perfect atmosphere, the perfect weather. I He had everything. He had a perfect relationship with the

Father. He had perfect understanding. He still chose to not obey his Father. But his Father said, "I've got a plan. When I send my son and I get these new sons, I'm going to, again, show them how to live from a place of rest."

Mercy people are designed for intimate relationships. They are sensitive to the emotional climate around them because they are wired for peace. John the Beloved was mercy. What did he say? "I'm the one Jesus loved. The Lord loved me." The picture you have of him at the Lord's supper has John laying his head on the Lord's chest. "He loves me." The exhorter's going, "Yeah, man, He loves *me*!" But the mercy is content to just rest with Jesus. That's why Mercies in worship can take us to a place with the Father that just exudes rest.

Mercy characteristics are that they make people feel accepted and safe. Intimacy is absolutely required and very easy. A mercy has got to feel connected. They will drive you insane until they feel a heart connection. If they don't feel like your heart is really connecting with them, they will pester you, they will badger you, they will drive you. When you're saying, "Everything's fine!" They'll be the one who says, "Nope, everything doesn't feel fine. That doesn't feel true. No, there's something wrong, I can just feel it." Why? They've got to feel that connection.

I'm finding that mercy people are word people. I don't know why that is, but mercy people want words. They want you to talk to them. They want to know how you feel. Or they want a lengthy letter written to them. They want communication. They want verbal communication with you to know how you feel. They want to help you get back to a place of rest and peace in relationships with people and with the Father.

Examples in scripture would be John, David, Ruth

John the Beloved was mercy. What did he say? "I'm the one Jesus loved. The Lord loved me." The picture you have of him at the Lord's supper has John laying his head on the Lord's chest. "He loves me." The exhorter's going, "Yeah, man, He loves *me*!" But the mercy is content to just rest with Jesus. That's why Mercies in worship can take us to a place with the Father that just exudes rest.

CHAPTER TEN

WHAT NOW

Understanding the design of each other is crucial, because look what's happened to us. We've all judged other people and how they think. We've all thought, "Well if *they* would *just*...Well if he would stop...Well if she would start...Well if they would do this...Well if he wasn't this..." Or we've thought they're doing it on purpose because they just want to be mean.

If we could start looking at this stuff and instead say, "Father I want to grow up." Everything we're talking about is based on the following: You want to change; you want to become like Jesus; you want to learn how to receive other people and walk in wholeness; you're willing for Him to show you the blind spots. If that's not the case, this is going to be knowledge you're going to gain and think, "Well that was fun. It wasn't a total waste of a day, but not sure it helped."

But like with anything else, if you want this to change your life, it can. If you want this to change you, relationally, it can. As I say, it's not an excuse to say, "Well it's just how I am. I'm just black and white. I just speak it the way it is. I have an opinion and I have a right to speak it whenever I want to. It's just how I'm wired." You can and sometimes do. But it doesn't always work out well when you just blurt out your opinion. However, if you will begin to look at it and say, "Lord, would you put a filter on me? Would you put the reins on me? Would you dial me down a little?"

I spent years trying to be quiet. People don't believe it, but that's because it never worked. Internally I was trying to be quiet and trying to be something I wasn't designed to be. It was tearing me up inside. Like a Servant man that's been put in a leadership role, he's not a natural leader and has no real innate desire to be. He tries and tries and tries but nothing works. Everyone runs over him. He just fails at everything rather than going, "Father this is how you've wired me, and if you want me to be a leader, then you're going to have to rise up within me to help me lead. Because I'm not going to lead the way anyone else does."

In spite of the wiring, the authority is by the presence of God, by *doing* it from a place of rest. If you're a servant and He asks you to lead, you can lead. If you're a Prophet, and He calls you to step back and be quiet, you can step back and be quiet. If you're a Ruler and what you really need to do is to be a Mercy because somebody needs the sensitivity and the feeling, you can step back and just go, "Come here. Let's just sit here and see what Jesus has to say about all this. Let's just rest."

Another thing I want you to see is that not only is this applicable outwardly between relationships, this is also applicable internally within ourselves.

In our soul man, in our mind, will, and emotions, we're seeing through our main gift. When I come to know Jesus in my spirit man, the fullness of who Jesus is, is born in me and I can now begin to reflect Him and mature and reflect more of who He is. That's sanctification. It's not an outward thing. It's an inward thing beginning to work out. Paul says, "Work out your own salvation." In other words, beginning to get in touch with the fullness of all seven Redemptive gifts that are within my spirit and maturing them so I can now mature into the image of Jesus. Truthfully, all that is in us cannot be measured, but by His mercy He gives us pictures of how to learn to walk and mature.

There have been times when I would ask this question. "What does it mean to look like Jesus?" Some would say, Be Loving, kind, do miracles. And then if I would ask, "How are you doing on that?" The answer would be, "Well, sometimes good, sometimes not so good."

We fully recognize specific characteristics of Jesus displayed in the Word, but we have no idea what

He was feeling, or thinking, or what internal struggles He had to resolve to do the will of His Father. Consequently, we don't really know what it means to reflect who Jesus is through us. Because we don't know who we are, and we've thought who we are is really not all that great, there is a significant disconnect in our attempts to draw a meaningful parallel. So, we've tried to change ourselves into an image that we can't even fully grasp the true essence of. We unconsciously struggle with the fact that Jesus didn't have to contend with the continual stress of dealing with the IRS, or car insurance, health insurance, a cell phone or the internet, not to mention a daily commute to an office … and we do. Everyday! We just don't have a grid for it, or a box to put it in.

I am not talking about our need for salvation or the struggle with the old nature, I am talking about the way God designed us. We have left society in chaos. We have left the world in chaos. We have left the church in chaos. But within us the spirit of God in here is saying, "If you will get to know me, if you will let me mature you and grow in your inner man and who I made you to be, you can reflect me. You can look like me. But allow me to mature you like I made you, not like I made someone else."

In conclusion I have incorporated some charts that show strengths (as maturity) and weaknesses (as carnal expressions) of characteristics of each gift.

As you go through them you will probably see yourself in several of the less mature areas, which is how we've been trained by our culture to see ourselves. Also, as you have begun to grow in Christ you will begin to reflect more of Him, consequently we are all somewhere between the two extremes of the chart. However, the fundamental lens through which you view life will still be the number one expression.

Understand, that all of these gifts are found in Jesus and because He dwells in us, we can begin to operate in a more balanced manner. Reflecting Him more fully, although we will always need each other.

A suggestion to begin the growth process is to take the list that most feels like you and begin to ask the Father where you do those things whether in weakness or in strength, or somewhere in between. Then begin to ask Him to Mature you in the weaknesses and thank Him for the strengths. He may show you responses you thought were wrong that simply need to be matured or others you thought were correct that He wants to change. Be open before Him. He truly wants you to walk in Freedom.

Remember. JESUS WANTS YOU TO BE THE YOU HE CREATED, SO HE CAN BE HIM THROUGH YOU.

ADDENDUM

Supernatural Reflection: Recognizing and Understanding Redemptive Gifts - Arizaga

Mature Prophet	Carnal Prophet
Release design and intent from the mind of God – correcting and restoring deficiencies, activating potential, future focused	Negative, hopeless, enemy manipulates their "design" gift to keep them focused on the problems/deficiencies around them, as well as things in the past, nursing grievances endlessly
Confronts sin boldly…but also has a vision for the fullness of God's grace, speaks with life-giving creative force "let there be light"!	Extremely critical /condemning pointing out what is wrong with everyone and everything…confronts without mercy, first in line to stone the sinner, dead right
Can forgive and extend mercy to self	Over-repents, has a tendency to extend forgiveness and mercy (when the responsibility for sin has been made ☺) to others but not self
Embraces the value of all God's principles, not content to arrive at fulfillment alone,	Gravitates only to personally likeable principles

55

encourages others to embrace pain and earn authority	
Embraces truths that deal with healthy relationship building	Often neglects truths that deal with healthy relationship building
Values growing in favor with God and man, has learned to endure hardships and persevere in difficult & unexplainable circumstances to earn natural and spiritual authority	Assigns blame, complains. Quits relationships, jobs, and churches, cannot persevere through seasons of preparation and impartation, they run ahead of God's Timing and try to initiate things on their own timing
Values and trusts God's timing, allows their root system to go deep in God, leaves the increase/results to God	Fear of being sidelined, has difficulty enduring pruning of God, especially when opportunities for successful ministry is removed
Embraces sonship, eradicating orphaned heart/thinking	Neglects the relational truths that deal with intimacy with God, tries to earn legitimacy and value by things he can do/has done

Responds appropriately to the situation while not limiting; God given emotional depth and capacity	Overreacts, extreme responses inappropriate to event
The prophet's birthright is to know the mind of God. They can see new applications of truth based on God's design and intent; this allows them to implement God's principles with the goal of rebuilding, repairing, and restoring.	Cannot possess their own birthright or empower other to reach theirs, usually isolated withdrawn, hopeless and wounded.

Mature Servant	Carnal Servant
Pursues intimacy/relationship with God	Uses religious activity & service to please God, performance oriented
Sees God as He is, sees themselves from His perspective, walks in true humility	Poor self-image, doesn't think that they matter as a person, embraces the victim spirit, walks in counterfeit humility
Speaks the truth in love, confronts, sets healthy boundaries	Martyrs, non-confrontational, complains so that others will set boundaries and confront for them
Embraces order, accepts personal responsibility, utilizes planning and organizational tools	Poor self-government, over commits, does too many things poorly rather than fewer things well, makes excuses
God-pleaser instead of man-pleaser, believes God's word about themselves, serves others while remaining "God oriented", attracts honor	Others-oriented, man-pleaser, believes what others say about them instead of what God says about them, they allow others to shape them by dishonorable, and slanderous comments, perpetuates dishonor

Leads others to cleansing and holiness	Enables poor character and dysfunctional behavior in others instead of empowering them to change
Serves their family in a "healthy way" providing opportunities for others to grow in personal responsibility	Denial regarding their children, usually meet too many of their children's needs. Make excuses for their children's bad character
Balanced, realistic expectations, anticipating the best but choosing to see things as they really are	Unrealistic, fairytale expectations, rejects reality, embraces "surreality"
Free to admit and learn from their mistakes, understands God's grace and compassion, knows that love is not earned	Have difficulty not defining themselves by their mistakes and breaking free from shame, perfectionism, low compassion (mercy for some – mercy for none)

Because of their trustworthiness and obedience God can trust the servant with unparalleled spiritual authority. Satan's only defense against them is to keep them from exercising their authority by never seeing themselves a God sees them, Mature servants can cleanse land, leaders, and have authority over premature death	Misunderstands true humility, and walks in poverty of spirit, thinking of themselves in self-deprecating, self-defeating terms. Passes the "work" of spiritual warfare to others they think are more "qualified"

Mature Teacher	Carnal Teacher
Relationship with truth	Values knowledge of God and religious service over relationship with God (looks for more credentials, degrees), arrogance and unhealthy confidence in knowledge
Values *rhema* logos and revelation	Values reason over revelation
Emotionally/passionately engages with God and others, values intimacy	Cerebral with God and others, not giving of self in relationships, false intimacy
Walks in the fullness of the responsibility principle	Selectively responsible, usually excelling at work, but negligent regarding home responsibilities and family holiness
Builds structures that steward new revelation	Accepts only what has been documented, ritual, "old wine'
As a Leader/Pastor/Parent, confronts sin in their midst	Carnal mercy, carnal love, and carnal guidance that enables sin and sinners; wants to love people into the kingdom – even after the time for repentance

	has passed (this heart attitude often causes Teachers to be confused with Mercies
Life-giving/healthy perspective regarding people, infrastructures, principles, and vision, etc.	Poor boundaries, poor future planning and preparation for growth, unbalanced ministry perspective
Releases truth that empowers and equips	Implements truth in a way that limits and controls others, sarcastic, condescending
Authority over predator spirit, protects those who are weak and wounded	Involved in their own "world" interests, takes two steps sideways or backwards instead of walking in the authority God has given them
Walks in healthy loyalty, can move on, in/with God mutually life-giving relationships	Unhealthy loyalty is perverted by the enemy to keep them in toxic relationships and environments

Birthright is to have access to "hidden manna" in the Word of God (they can bring out of the storehouse of the Word the old and the new truth combined). This hidden manna also pertains to supernatural intercessory strategies	Rejects undocumented truth and spiritual experiences having confidence in "what" they know instead of "who they know.

Mature Exhorter	Carnal Exhorter
Controls their time - pulls back from social activities and the horizontal relationships – allocates significant amounts of time alone in order to get to know God, His word	Has good intentions but lacks self-government, time management
Reveals God to people – brings the knowledge of God, shows people their God, His nature	Focuses on tasks and visions, inspires and mobilizes people to participate in activities and plans rather than mobilizing them around the purposes of God
Mobilizes, influences, and inspires people to reach their full potential in God	Uses influence to achieve their personal agenda and goals
Has earned authority/incarnate truth that came by persevering through and embracing pain and suffering in them lives	Unwilling to embrace pain/suffering and trials as God's gift to us in order to "know" Him, grow character
Embraces pain of personal and relational healing	Uses tasks and projects to distracts themselves

Has life-giving, transparent relationships	Disconnects from painful relationships, has superficial, sometimes self-serving relationships
Brings balance to the other gifts, reveals missing truth, expands revelation, "stirs things up"	Can mobilize and gather people, but has nothing to deposit
Governs by principle, God-pleaser (secure identity), values input and exchange from other gifts	Governs by relationship rather than by principle/more concerned about the approval of people (man-pleasing), over-sensitive to rejection and reaction from inside the "camp"
Confronts sin in due season	Unwilling to confront sin in the "camp" to keep from experiencing rejection – fails to confront sin in the camp in due season
Embraces self-government, operates in established administrative systems, recognizes weakness, solution-oriented	Doesn't want to reap the natural consequences God designed to discipline their poor judgment, administration and leadership – an extension of the unwillingness to embrace

65

	pain and suffering
Their birthright is to have influence over significant numbers of people by revealing the nature of God to them, has influence over cities and nations, which inspires and mobilizes them into the purposes of God	Lack of control of their time – spends too much time on the horizontal relationships and not enough time being alone with God – this is why Exhorters fail to possess their birthright more than any other Gifts

Mature Giver	Carnal Giver
Gives wisely to establish ministries in their time of abundance and in their time of need	Gives only in time of abundance
Trusts God to deliver what He has promised, has learned to trust God and takes financial risks based on faith instead of always waiting for the safe deal	Overly cautions, decisions based on fear rather than faith, can't birth new things
Balanced generosity – stands against the destructive forces of excess and indulgence	Too frugal with family members, or generous with an intent to control
Dependent on God, walks in strong relationship with God instead of relying on themselves – this is result of walking through some significant testing that was designed to teach the Giver	Independent to the extreme, tries to live independent of God - this lack of relationship can cause the carnal Giver to walk in fear and mistrust

Trusts God, sees themselves as a conduit of blessing	Puts trust and security in money/possessions, does not see themselves a as a conduit; hoards, puts trust in the extended family
No longer uses religious activity to please God but walks in a true love (heartfelt) relationship, embraces "new wine"	Walks out their faith like a business contract, keeping their "end of the bargain," prefers tradition and liturgy
Develops life-giving relationship within immediate family	Uses unhealthy, emotional manipulations to control family members, petty
Builds/provides for the future based on faith	Suspicious, fearful of what might happened, builds protective "structures" based on fear
Walks in holiness/not casual about God's absolutes	Doesn't accept God's absolutes/wants to keep their options open
Accepts responsibility for past mistakes, willing to make amends, acknowledges unhealthy patterns	Does not learn from the past well, makes same mistakes over and over but considers each situation as unique and different, resents being confronted about pattern, mistakes, or things from the past

| Their authority enables them to utilize their birthright to impart generational blessings of wealth and favor | Scrooge |

Mature Ruler	Carnal Ruler
Applies pressure with wisdom for short periods of time to meet certain productive goals	Applies constant pressure to the work/ministry/home environment
High moral integrity, leads by principle, will take a stand for righteousness regardless of the personal	Walks in moral compromise, thinking that their great works/accomplishments are enough to compensate
Completes tasks with excellence	Completes tasks 80%, disregards 20%
Shares authority and leadership with others; team player, can partner with other churches for citywide group efforts to evangelize, capacity to restore co-regent (male/female dominion)	Self-reliant, doesn't see the need to partner with others, takes credit for results without recognizing/valuing the contributions of others
Leads others in a life-giving manner, doesn't push people beyond their limits; Aaron's Rod, builds Kingdom and nurtures people	Leads or governs others by control & exploitation, over-administrates, is more concerned with meeting "the goal" and finishing the project by deadline than with the people

	involved in the project
Has life healthy relationships	Task and responsibility oriented, doesn't nurture the key relationships in their lives, "Great Commission" over "Greatest Commandment"
Makes time for relationship building, engages emotionally	During times of family & relational stress will work more to avoid problems
Completes the key task God has given them, no longer busy and distracted by the multiple interests and abilities they have, they do the "God-thing" instead of all the "good things"	Is too busy with the multiple interests and activities to complete key projects, driven by the desire to do more and more, endlessly pursuing more objectives
Has learned to partner with God – because of this partnership they can get results that are disproportionate to the amount of resources they have – can build and maintain significant ministries with very limited resources	Finds their valued in work and accomplishments, instead of in God

Draws balance, correction from the other gifts, allows the Holy Spirit to reveal hidden faults	Thinks they are right, can't receive corrections, will have power confrontations to convince others they are right
The Ruler is the empire builder; it is their birthright to impart generational blessings to government systems, kingdoms, and nations. They are specifically anointed to impart blessing on people's spiritual walk. In spiritual warfare they have authority over unjust, abuse, and righteousness	Judges others, draws righteousness to themselves, "elder brother" syndrome, love of law over law of love

Mature Mercy	Carnal Mercy
Makes decisions based on Godly principles & values combined with the heart of God for themselves and others	Does not stand on values but does whatever necessary to make people around them happy. Leads and makes decisions based on feelings
Walks in genuine mercy and judgment, embraces discipline and pain as part of the healing/ growing process	Flees pain and the discipline of God, protects others from the appropriate negative consequences, cannot discern counterfeit mercy from genuine mercy
Walks in true empathy to lead others to healing and repentance with wisdom and appropriate boundaries	Embraces dangerous people who do not demonstrate 'fruit meet for repentance', often won't leave jobs, churches, relationships that are exploitive, victim mindset justifies why it is "right for them to do wrong"
Observes appropriate boundaries, keeps rank	Takes up offense for a third party, gets involved where they don't belong

Draws balance from other gifts, has learned to respond rather than react	Mishandles/misapplies their discernment, overreacts
Disciplines consistently avoiding emotional extremes, allows children to suffer appropriate negative consequences	Doesn't allow appropriate component of "suffering" in the discipline of their children, thinks love alone is enough
God-pleasing, free from the fear of man	Wrapped up in the opinions of men, man-pleasing
Has resolved their identity issues, their identity is based in relationship with the Father, has true emotional wholeness, has allowed God to re-father them and bring healing to their hearts, can confront sin with love	Passes the buck, won't take a stand on issues, indecisive when crucial decisions need to be made, fearful, insecure, cannot risk, chameleon, won't confront sin
Have found true fulfillment in the spirit-to- spirit connection with God; because of this level of fulfillment and interfacing with God's Spirit, Mercies can actually bring the	Inappropriate intimacy, pursues self- gratification in all forms, does not have clear emotional identity, cannot walk freely in their dominion, blames external circumstances for

"glory" out of the Holy Place and can transfer/release that glory to families & situations. When walking in mature holiness, can sanctify time	agitated state, stays needy rather than becoming life-giving
Displays God's heart, His true redemptive plan for man, embraces God's mind, God's ways, God's truth, along with God's heart. Recognizes there is no true mercy without judgment	Motivated by fear and feelings, walks in counterfeit/immature fruit of the spirit enabling corruption, defilement, "plays for the wrong team", enables counterfeit unity and rebellion

About the Author

Pat Banks, the youngest of four children, was born and raised in Kansas. Her father got saved later in life, while she was in Grade School, and within a couple of years surrendered to go into full-time ministry. She graduated High School in Sharon Springs, KS and shortly thereafter moved to Fort Worth, TX to take on the world. Following a move to Houston, she enrolled in college and began working for Southwestern Bell Telephone. It wasn't long before she became an executive trainer for the company.

In late 1979 she met Jim Banks and they were married the following year, moving immediately to Indianapolis, Indiana where she resumed her career with Southwestern Bell. From that point until they entered ministry full time, they ministered on nights and weekends, leading small groups, discipling and teaching Bible studies. After raising four children and following a move from the Atlanta area to Asheville, NC in 2002 they decided to leave the corporate world for good. Ministry has been their sole focus ever since. Jim and Pat now live in the Nashville, Tennessee area.

Pat is still "a trainer," a teacher, a public speaker, an inner healing and deliverance minister, and now an author, dedicated to loving God and loving people.

Made in the USA
Columbia, SC
03 March 2025